INSPIRATION TO GET YOU THROUGH A F🌷CKED UP YEAR

ARON GAUDET + GITA PULLAPILLY

This publication contains the opinions and ideas of its authors. It is intended to provide helpful and informative material on the subjects addressed in the publication. It is sold with the understanding that the authors and publisher are not engaged in rendering psychological/mental health, medical, or any other kind of personal professional services in the book. The reader should consult his or her medical, or mental health care professional, or other competent professional before adopting any of the suggestions in the book or drawing inferences from it. The authors and publisher specifically disclaim all responsibility for any liability, loss or risk, personal, or otherwise, which is incurred as a consequence, directly or indirectly, of the use and application of any of the contents of this book.

Cross Cultural
PUBLICATIONS

Acknowledgements

We wish to thank the Gaudet & Pullapilly families for their support. Our friends, Leo & Lisa Doyle, Mark & Claire Haidar, Kayla Emter & Martin Bernfeld, Jane Schoettle, Ellie Lee, Dr. Joseph Sakran, Dr. Adeeti Gupta, and countless others who didn't think we were crazy to spend a year writing inspirational quotes.

We'd also like to thank all of the people who have made us suffer over this past year. Without you, we wouldn't have learned all of these valuable lessons that made us stronger, braver, kinder, and better.

Book Team

Editor:	Carol Varney
Assistant Editor:	Gef Gove
Illustrator:	Andrii Protsiuk
Graphic Designer:	Bansari Desai
Book Designer:	Marie Stirk

This book is dedicated to
Joan Gaudet and Dr. Cyriac Pullapilly. Two people who
went above and beyond to share their love, kindness,
and compassion with strangers around the world.
You will be forever missed.

Preface

We work in Hollywood. It can be a cutthroat business filled with ego, jealousy, and superficiality. How have we survived—and even thrived—in this environment? We sought counsel from people considered to be the "best leaders" around the world—top therapists, highest-ranking military personnel, and most compassionate religious and spiritual scholars. We asked them to help us develop the mental "tools" necessary to get us through all the ups and downs in life. Over the years, they have inspired us. They have helped us fill our mental toolbox, so we can face life's challenges head on.

Dealing with everyday problems in life never ends. You may solve one problem, but it will simply be replaced by another. The key is to become stronger and more resilient in the *solving* of each new problem. In the same vein, suffering never ends, and suffering cannot be avoided. But if you can learn to embrace the suffering and turn it into fertilizer, then you can grow to become a better friend, a better partner, and a better human being.

We started to approach each new week not with dread, but rather, with a question: "What's in our toolbox to help us get through the difficult tasks we are facing?" From that question, an experiment was born. We have always been motivated by inspirational quotes. What if we created our own inspiring quotes, each week, for an entire year? Quotes that summed up what motivated us, or guided us, to get through the challenges of that particular week.

First, we would need a couple of rules:

1. We committed to focusing on our toolbox and applying these tools to our everyday lives for *52 straight weeks*. We vowed to not miss a single week. This was much harder than we anticipated.

2. We decided to share these quotes unvarnished. We didn't polish them up for you. We are sharing them in the order they occurred in our life. Some weeks weren't so bad. Others were hard as fuck. Just like life.

At the root of many of life's challenges there is a pattern. Our weaknesses and triggers don't just disappear after one week; they repeat themselves over and over again. Conquering them takes time. Somtimes we must play "whack a mole" with our flaws, until they stop rearing their ugly heads. Just recognizing this is growth!

Our challenge to you: can you tackle one quote a week for 52 weeks? It's not how quickly you read through the quotes; it's what you do with each one over those seven days. How do you put these thoughts into action? Can you learn to nurture yourself with love and compassion? We believe that if you do, eventually you will see the seeds of personal growth blossom into a beautiful flower.

What began as random thoughts evolved into something that truly changed us. When all was said and done, we realized we got through a fucked up year with kindness, compassion, integrity, and growth. We are sharing our 52 quotes in the hope that this year will be equally profound and moving for you, despite the obstacles you will face. *And there will be many.*

Instructions On Using This Book

1. This book isn't precious. We encourage you to WRITE IN IT and RIP OUT your favorite quotes. It's a tool in your toolbox to get you through the year.

2. Take it one week at a time. You will make progress. You don't have to be your best self every week. Over the year, if you start seeing your words and actions overlap, well damn, the book is working!

3. Remember, you are LOVED. You are important. You are precious. Thank you for trying to make this world a better place. Now, let's get started.

UNCONDITIONAL LOVE, UNCONDITIONAL FORGIVENESS. IT COMES SO EASY FOR DOGS, SO HARD FOR HUMANS.

OKAY, YOU'RE THINKING, "WHAT THE HELL?!
THIS IS THE FIRST QUOTE? HOW ABOUT SOME INSPIRATION?!"
BEFORE WE CAN INSPIRE, WE NEED TO REFLECT. WE KNOW DOGS
ARE AMAZING, BUT WHAT ABOUT US HUMANS? ON A SCALE OF
1-10, WITH 10 BEING **MOST AMAZING**, WHERE WOULD YOU RATE
YOURSELF ON BEING A GOOD HUMAN? ...AND WHY? BE HONEST.
THIS IS YOUR STARTING POINT AND THE GOAL IS TO GET
BETTER EACH AND EVERY WEEK.

WE GET IT. THIS IS STARTING TO FEEL LIKE A TRUST TEST. SO, TRUST US. IF WE ALL CAN'T RECOGNIZE THE FLAWS OR MISTAKES WE ARE MAKING ON EARTH, THEN WHAT'S THE POINT OF GROWING AND GETTING BETTER? WRITE DOWN SOME OF YOUR CONCERNS ABOUT THIS PLANET. IF YOU COULD RUN THE WORLD, WHAT WOULD YOU DO TO MAKE IT BETTER (BESIDES MORE DOGS, OBVIOUSLY)?

BURYING OUR EMOTIONS IS LIKE PLANTING A SEED. IT ONLY MAKES OUR ANGER AND PAIN GROW. RELEASE IT AND LET IT BLOW AWAY LIKE THE WIND.

ARE YOU FEELING STRESSED, SAD, OVERWHELMED, ANGRY, ANNOYED, OR FRUSTRATED? IF SO, WHY? WRITE IT ALL DOWN. ACKNOWLEDGE YOUR EMOTIONS AND RELEASE THEM FROM YOUR BODY. LET THEM GO. ANY NEGATIVE EMOTIONS ARE TOXINS. GET THEM OUT OF YOUR SYSTEM PRONTO.

WEEK 4

PAY ATTENTION!
INSPIRATION CAN BE FOUND
IN THE MOST UNLIKELY
PLACES.

WRITE DOWN YOUR GOALS FOR THE DAY...
FOR THE WEEK... FOR THE MONTH... AND FOR THE YEAR.
THEN, WHISPER WHAT YOU WROTE TO YOURSELF.
NOW, SAY IT LOUDER. FINALLY, WHEN YOU GO OUT INTO THE
WORLD, LOOK FOR ALL THE SIGNS AND MESSAGES THAT THE
UNIVERSE IS GIVING YOU. LET THE WORLD INSPIRE YOU, LIFT
YOU UP, AND GUIDE YOU TOWARD YOUR GOALS.

EVERY DAY WE JUST HAVE TO GO OUT THERE AND DO OUR BEST. THE REST IS OUT OF OUR CONTROL.

WHAT IS **IN YOUR CONTROL** AS YOU
WORK TO ACHIEVE YOUR GOALS THIS WEEK?
WRITE IT DOWN. TAPE IT TO YOUR DESK OR NEAR YOUR
COMPUTER. WHAT YOU HOPE TO ACHIEVE IS POSSIBLE WITH
SELF-DISCIPLINE AND A GOOD ROUTINE. YOU MAY NOT
ACHIEVE EVERY GOAL IN ONE WEEK, BUT OPPORTUNITIES WILL
ARISE IF YOU ARE PREPARED FOR THEM.

IT'S A BEAUTIFUL THING TO
BE LOVED BY PEOPLE WHO ONLY WANT
THE BEST FOR YOU. FINDING REAL
FRIENDS IS HARD. BUT WHEN YOU DO,
YOU HAVE THEM FOR LIFE.

THINK ABOUT THE PEOPLE WHO WERE THERE FOR YOU WHEN YOU FACED AN ENORMOUS STRUGGLE, A LOSS OF SOME KIND, A CHALLENGING RELATIONSHIP, OR A HEALTH SCARE. EACH PERSON WAS THERE BECAUSE THEY LOVED YOU AND CARED FOR YOU. YOU ARE AN IMPORTANT PERSON IN THEIR LIFE. INSTEAD OF WRITING ABOUT THEM HERE, WRITE A NOTE TO THEM. TELL THEM HOW MUCH IT MEANS TO YOU TO HAVE THEM IN YOUR LIFE. TAKE THE TIME TO TELL EACH OF THESE PEOPLE HOW MUCH YOU VALUE AND APPRECIATE THEM. TOMORROW IS NOT GUARANTEED, BUT YOU HAVE TODAY.

FEAR IS OUR ENEMY. FEAR HOLDS US BACK.
WE MUST REMOVE FEAR AND REPLACE IT WITH POSITIVE
ENERGY AND A PLAN. WRITE DOWN WHAT YOU'RE DREADING
MOST THIS WEEK. THEN, WRITE DOWN THE STEPS YOU ARE
GOING TO TAKE TO CONQUER THIS PROBLEM, AS WELL AS A
STRATEGY THAT WILL PROTECT YOU BOTH EMOTIONALLY
AND PHYSICALLY.

BIRTHDAYS ARE A TIME TO REFLECT ON THE YEAR THAT PASSED, AND VISUALIZE ALL YOUR HOPES FOR THE YEAR TO COME.

NOT YOUR BIRTHDAY THIS WEEK?
SAVE THIS EXERCISE FOR WHEN IT IS.
THINK ABOUT THE LAST YEAR OF YOUR LIFE. WHAT
REGRETS DO YOU HAVE? WHAT CAN YOU DO DIFFERENTLY
TO MAKE THIS YEAR BETTER THAN THE LAST?
MAKE THIS A YEAR OF GROWTH!

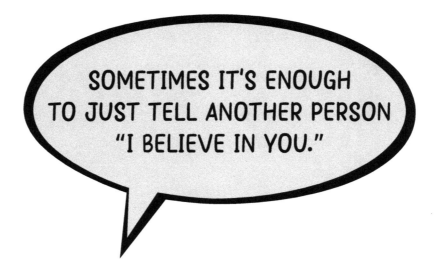

IN THE SAME WAY YOU HAVE DOUBTS, SO DO YOUR
FRIENDS, FAMILY, AND COLLEAGUES. THINK ABOUT
SOMEONE IN YOUR LIFE WHO IS GOING THROUGH A TOUGH
TIME RIGHT NOW. TELL THEM WHY YOU BELIEVE IN THEM.
SOMETIMES A FEW WORDS IS ALL IT TAKES TO INSPIRE
SOMEONE TO KEEP FIGHTING FOR ANOTHER DAY.
WE BELIEVE THAT YOU CAN DO THIS!

THERE'S A BIG DIFFERENCE
BETWEEN BEING FULL OF PRIDE
AND BEING PRIDEFUL.
WHICH ARE YOU?

EGO IS NOT YOUR AMIGO.
BE PROUD OF THE THINGS YOU'VE ACCOMPLISHED,
BUT DON'T LET THEM GO TO YOUR HEAD.
WRITE DOWN THE ACCOMPLISHMENTS FROM THE PAST WEEK
THAT YOU'RE MOST PROUD OF. PAT YOURSELF ON THE BACK.
NOW REMEMBER, YOU CAN ALWAYS DO BETTER. WHAT ARE
YOUR BIG GOALS FOR THIS WEEK?

WEEK 11

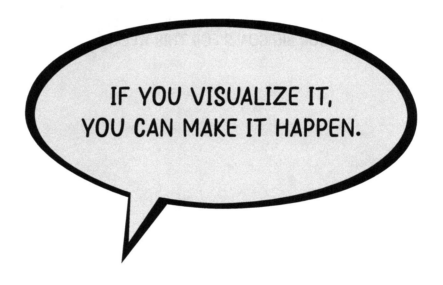

WRITE DOWN A GOAL YOU PLAN TO ACCOMPLISH
THIS WEEK. WRITE IT DOWN FIVE TIMES. THEN SAY IT
FIVE TIMES IN YOUR HEAD. NOW CLOSE YOUR EYES AND
VISUALIZE YOURSELF ACCOMPLISHING THIS GOAL.
WALK THROUGH EACH AND EVERY STEP IT WILL TAKE.
WHAT DOES IT FEEL LIKE WHEN YOU ACHIEVE YOUR GOAL?
STAY IN THIS MOMENT. **WILL THIS MOMENT INTO REALITY.**

WE SHOULD ALL STRIVE TO LEAVE EVERY HUMAN INTERACTION HOPING WE HAVE MADE THE OTHER PERSON BETTER.

WHEN WE MAKE OTHER PEOPLE FEEL BETTER,
WE FEEL BETTER OURSELVES. WHO ARE YOU GOING TO MAKE
FEEL BETTER TODAY? HOW CAN YOU GO OUT OF YOUR WAY
TO MAKE SOMEONE LAUGH, SMILE, OR FEEL SPECIAL? THIS IS
A "GET OUT OF YOUR COMFORT ZONE" EXERCISE. GO FOR IT.
MAKE IT HAPPEN. ONE DAY YOU COULD BE THE PERSON ON
THE OTHER END OF THIS ACTION AND YOU'LL APPRECIATE THE
THOUGHTFUL GESTURE.

INSTEAD OF BLAMING SOMEONE IN THE FACE OF FAILURE, WHAT IF WE ASK OURSELVES, "WHAT MORE COULD I HAVE DONE TO HELP THEM SUCCEED?"

THERE WILL ALWAYS BE FAILURES IN LIFE.
WE COUNT ON PEOPLE AND THEY CAN OFTEN DISAPPOINT.
IT'S FRUSTRATING AND EASY TO PLAY THE BLAME GAME.
BUT INSTEAD OF PLACING BLAME, A REAL LEADER WILL
STEP BACK AND ASK, "WHAT MORE COULD I HAVE DONE TO
ENSURE SUCCESS?" MOST TIMES, YOU WILL RECOGNIZE
INSTANCES WHEN YOU COULD HAVE INTERVENED EARLIER.
NOW, WRITE DOWN HOW YOU ARE GOING TO PLAN FOR
SUCCESS THE NEXT TIME.

DON'T SAY "NO" TO AN OPPORTUNITY BEFORE IT HAS TIME TO FULLY BLOOM. A THORNY IDEA CAN STILL TURN INTO A ROSE.

THE BEST OPPORTUNITIES OFTEN COME WITH THE MOST RISKS. THEY MAY TAKE A LONG TIME TO DEVELOP AND THERE'S ALWAYS A CHANCE THEY WON'T WORK OUT. IF YOU'RE UNSURE OF AN OPPORTUNITY, WRITE DOWN THE NEXT STEPS IN PURSUING IT. TAKE THIS WEEK TO EXPLORE THOSE STEPS IN A MEANINGFUL WAY. REASSESS AT THE END OF THE WEEK. DO YOU HAVE A NEW PERSPECTIVE ON THIS OPPORTUNITY?

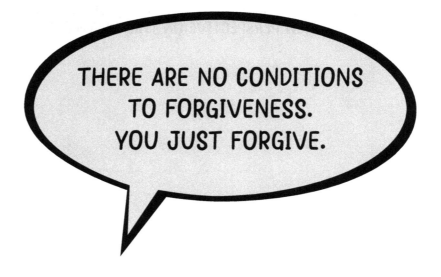

HAS SOMEONE SCREWED WITH YOU THIS WEEK AND LEFT YOU WANTING REVENGE? THE NATURAL RESPONSE IS TO WANT THEM TO SUFFER AS THEY HAVE MADE YOU SUFFER. BUT WHY NOT TRY FORGIVENESS INSTEAD? MOST PHONES HAVE A VOICE RECORDER. PRESS RECORD AND PRETEND THAT PERSON IS ON THE OTHER END. SAY EVERYTHING YOU NEED TO SAY TO THIS PERSON. SCREAM IT IF YOU NEED TO. LET THEM KNOW EXACTLY HOW THEY HURT YOU, BETRAYED YOU, NEGLECTED YOU, OR POSSIBLY DESTROYED YOU. AT THE VERY END OF THIS RECORDING SAY, "I FORGIVE YOU [NAME OF PERSON]." GO TAKE A SHOWER. WASH ALL THE NEGATIVITY AWAY. NOW, COME BACK TO YOUR PHONE. DON'T LISTEN TO THE RECORDING. <u>JUST DELETE IT</u>. <u>DELETE</u>. <u>DELETE</u>. <u>DELETE</u>. MAKE SURE THE RECORDING IS GONE. NOW CARRY ON WITH FORGIVENESS IN YOUR HEART. IF THIS PERSON STILL MAKES YOU SIMMER WITH RAGE, WE LOVE TO USE THE HAWAIIAN PRACTICE OF "HO'OPONOPONO." IT'S A BEAUTIFUL RECONCILIATION AND FORGIVENESS TECHNIQUE THAT REALLY WORKS!

BE THANKFUL FOR THE AIR
YOU BREATHE AND THE LOVE
YOU GIVE AND RECEIVE.

CONGRATULATIONS! YOU ARE ALIVE.
YOU ARE NOT ALONE. YOU ARE IMPORTANT TO OTHERS. YOU
ARE APPRECIATED AND VALUED. EVERY MORNING THIS WEEK,
LOOK AT YOURSELF IN THE MIRROR AND SAY OUT LOUD:
"I AM PRECIOUS. I AM LOVED." REPEAT THIS FIVE TIMES.
NOW YOU ARE MORE OPEN TO RECEIVE LOVE.

IF TRIALS AND TRIBULATIONS ARE SUPPOSED TO SHAPE US, THEN WE'RE ALL JUST WALKING MYRIAGONS.

IN GEOMETRY, A MYRIAGON IS A POLYGON WITH 10,000 SIDES. EACH TIME WE SUFFER IN LIFE WE ARE ADDING ANOTHER SIDE TO OUR SHAPE. WE CANNOT AVOID SUFFERING. THERE IS NO ESCAPING IT. A BUDDHIST MONK EXPLAINED TO US THAT WE MUST EMBRACE SUFFERING. WE MUST TURN OUR SUFFERING INTO COMPOST. WE MUST USE OUR SUFFERING TO GROW. THINK ABOUT THE LAST TIME YOU TRULY SUFFERED. WRITE DOWN WHAT YOU LEARNED FROM THAT EXPERIENCE. HOW HAS IT HELPED YOU GROW?

YOUR POSITIVE ENERGY
IS A VALUABLE RESOURCE.
DON'T LET OTHERS
STEAL IT FROM YOU.

POSITIVE ENERGY POWERS US THROUGH LIFE.
WRITE DOWN THE NAME OF A PERSON WHO CREATES DRAMA
AND/OR TENSION IN YOUR LIFE. HOW MUCH TIME DO YOU
SPEND WITH THAT PERSON? DOES YOUR TIME SPENT WITH
THAT PERSON DRAIN YOU OF YOUR POSITIVITY?
BRAINSTORM WAYS YOU CAN RATION YOUR TIME WITH THIS
INDIVIDUAL AND CONSERVE YOUR POSITIVE ENERGY.

LIFE WILL NEVER GO AS PLANNED.
HOW CAN WE MAKE THAT A POSITIVE? TAKE TIME
THIS WEEK TO FIND MOMENTS TO EXPLORE THE WORLD
AWAY FROM YOUR HOUSE, YOUR OFFICE, YOUR PHONE.
TAKE A WALK. VISIT A PLACE YOU'VE NEVER BEEN.
BE SPONTANEOUS. JUST GO. NO EXCUSES. USE YOUR
LUNCH BREAK. GET UP AN HOUR EARLIER THAN USUAL.
GO TO BED AN HOUR LATER. REFRESH YOUR MIND AND
RE-ENERGIZE YOUR CREATIVITY. YOU WILL SURPRISE
YOURSELF AT WHAT YOU DISCOVER ALONG THE WAY.

BE GRATEFUL FOR THE
TIME YOU HAVE WITH OTHERS,
FOR SOON IT WILL ALL
BE GONE.

THINK BACK TO THE BEST MOMENTS OF YOUR LIFE.
WHO WAS THERE? WHO HAVE YOU LAUGHED WITH?
WHO DID A CRAZY THING WITH YOU? WHO BAILED YOU OUT
OF A TOUGH SPOT? WHO IS GOING TO SHATTER YOUR WORLD
WHEN THEY ARE GONE? MAKE THE TIME TO CONNECT WITH
THEM THIS WEEK AND TELL THEM HOW MUCH YOU
LOVE AND APPRECIATE THEM.

YOUR WORD IS THE MOST VALUABLE COMMODITY YOU
HAVE. WHEN YOU MAKE A PROMISE, DO YOU KEEP IT?
WHAT HAVE YOU PROMISED TO DO RECENTLY?
WHAT WILL YOU NEED TO DO TO MAKE THAT PROMISE
A REALITY? WRITE IT DOWN, RIP THIS PAGE OUT, TAPE IT
WHERE YOU'LL SEE IT EACH DAY, AND GET ON IT!

THERE IS TOO MUCH NOISE IN THE WORLD. WE RARELY
HAVE ANY MEANINGFUL QUIET TIME. WRITE THE WORD "OFF"
IN BIG BLOCK LETTERS IN THE SPACE BELOW. NOW CARVE OUT
QUIET TIME THIS WEEK. THIS COULD MEAN MEDITATING, OR
JUST SITTING IN A ROOM, THINKING THROUGH YOUR
PROBLEMS WITHOUT DISTRACTION.

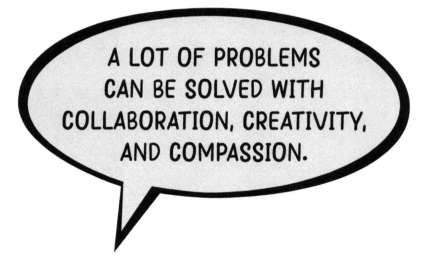

YOU DON'T HAVE ALL THE ANSWERS. WE DON'T HAVE ALL THE ANSWERS. BUT SOMEONE AROUND YOU WILL HAVE INSIGHT ON THE PROBLEM YOU'RE CURRENTLY STRUGGLING WITH. DROP THE EGO AND ASK FOR HELP. GET CREATIVE. LISTEN TO OTHERS. DEEPLY LISTEN. YOU'LL LIKELY FIND AN ANSWER IN THE LEAST EXPECTED PLACE.

A SMALL GESTURE,
MADE WITH LOVE, CAN HAVE A
BIG IMPACT ON THE ONE
RECEIVING IT.

WHAT COULD YOU DO THIS WEEK TO SHOW KINDNESS TO
A STRANGER? MAKE A LIST AND TRY ONE OUT. GET EXCITED.
YOU'RE GOING TO LOVE DOING THIS MORE OFTEN!

IF YOU HAVE TROUBLE
FORGIVING SOMEONE, YOU SHOULD
TRY FORGIVING YOURSELF FIRST.
HEALING COMES FROM WITHIN.

BACK TO FORGIVENESS. WE ALL MAKE MISTAKES.
PEOPLE HURT PEOPLE. SOMETIMES IT IS MALICIOUS, BUT OFTEN IT
IS NOT. DRAW A BIG HEART IN THE SPACE BELOW AND WRITE YOUR
NAME INSIDE OF IT. NOW CLOSE YOUR EYES. TALK TO YOURSELF.
FORGIVE YOURSELF FOR WHATEVER MISTAKES YOU HAVE MADE.
FORGIVE YOURSELF FOR HURTING OTHERS. FORGIVE YOURSELF
SO YOU CAN CARRY ON AND SAY, "I LOVE YOU AND FORGIVE YOU,
[THE PERSON YOU FORGIVE]."

NOTE: THERE ARE NEVER ENOUGH TOOLS TO
HELP US WITH FORGIVENESS.

OUR NEW MANTRA:
I AM GETTING BETTER
AND BETTER EACH DAY
IN EVERY ASPECT OF MY
LIFE.

CONGRATULATIONS!
YOU'RE HALFWAY THROUGH A YEAR OF HEALING AND
GROWTH. YOU ARE MAKING PROGRESS DAY BY DAY, WEEK BY
WEEK. IN THE SPACE BELOW, WRITE DOWN THE PHRASE,
"POCKET THE WIN." EVEN SMALL VICTORIES CAN BE MAJOR
"WINS." EVERY TIME YOU MAKE PROGRESS, TAKE A MOMENT TO
"POCKET THE WIN." WHAT ARE THREE "WINS" WORTH
POCKETING FROM THIS PAST WEEK?

THE ONLY THING YOU CAN CONTROL IS YOUR BREATH. BREATHE DEEPLY. IT WILL BE OKAY.

WE TAKE BREATHING FOR GRANTED, BUT IT IS A POWERFUL
TOOL TO CALM OURSELVES AND HEAL OUR BODY. WHEN YOU
FOCUS ON YOUR BREATHING IN AN INTENTIONAL WAY YOU CAN
CONTROL YOUR EMOTIONS, IMPROVE YOUR FOCUS, AND BEGIN
TO HEAL. TAKE FIVE MINUTES TO INHALE AND EXHALE.
KEEP YOUR MOUTH CLOSED AND INHALE DEEPLY. FEEL YOUR
BREATH TRAVELING FROM THE TIP OF YOUR NOSE TO THE
BOTTOM OF YOUR TOES. SLOWLY EXHALE FROM THE BOTTOM
OF YOUR TOES TO THE TIP OF YOUR NOSE.
INHALE. STAY CALM. EXHALE. GATHER YOUR THOUGHTS.
KEEP BREATHING. YOU WILL BE OKAY.

IF ANOTHER HUMAN
HAS DONE IT,
YOU HAVE THE POWER
TO DO IT, TOO.

CHANGE IS THE ONLY CONSTANT. HUMANS ARE ALWAYS ADAPTING. THE LIMITS OF WHAT WE ALL BELIEVE HUMANS CAN ACHIEVE KEEPS EXPANDING. WHO IS YOUR ROLE MODEL FOR ACHIEVING A GOAL YOU'VE SET FOR YOURSELF? WHAT STEPS DID THEY TAKE TO SUCCEED? CAN YOU TAKE THEIR PATH AND ADAPT IT TO BECOME YOUR OWN ROADMAP?

IN THIS WORLD, THERE ARE PEOPLE WHO CARE ONLY FOR THEMSELVES. YOU WILL ENCOUNTER THESE PEOPLE EVERY DAY, AND YOU MAY NOT ALWAYS RECOGNIZE THEM FOR WHO THEY ARE. BUT IF YOU LIVE YOUR CORE VALUES AND ARE GENUINE, KIND, AND HELPFUL TO OTHERS, YOUR FRIENDS WILL BE THERE FOR YOU WHEN IT COUNTS. WRITE DOWN THE NAMES OF YOUR THREE CLOSEST FRIENDS. HOW CAN YOU SHOW THEM THAT YOU APPRECIATE AND VALUE THEM?

WHAT LOOKS LIKE LUCK IS OFTEN YEARS OF PLANTING SEEDS AND WAITING FOR THEM TO GROW.

WRITE DOWN ALL THE MAJOR CHOICES AND DECISIONS
YOU MADE TO GET TO WHERE YOU ARE RIGHT NOW. THEN,
PLOT OUT THE NEXT TEN STEPS TO GET YOU WHERE YOU
WANT TO BE NEXT YEAR AT THIS TIME. NOW ASK YOURSELF,
"WHAT'S STOPPING ME FROM TACKLING STEP ONE?"

IN SEARCH OF BALANCE,
YOU'LL NEVER REGRET CHOOSING
LIFE OVER WORK.

HOW MUCH TIME HAVE YOU SET ASIDE THIS WEEK FOR SELF-CARE, AND RELATIONSHIP CULTIVATION AND MAINTENANCE? ARE YOU MAKING TIME TO MEDITATE, EXERCISE, READ (FROM AN ACTUAL BOOK), AND SPEND QUALITY TIME WITH FAMILY AND FRIENDS? OPEN YOUR CALENDAR AND START BLOCKING OFF "FRIEND TIME," "FAMILY TIME," "QUIET TIME," "EXERCISE," ETC. YOU ARE AT YOUR BEST WHEN YOU INVEST IN YOURSELF AND YOUR OWN WELL-BEING.

HOW MUCH MORE CONFIDENT DO YOU FEEL WHEN YOU ARE PREPARED TO MEET THE MOMENT? PEOPLE WHO REPEATEDLY RISE TO THE OCCASION ARE THE SAME PEOPLE WHO PLAN, PRACTICE, AND PREPARE BEFORE THEY EXECUTE. WRITE DOWN YOUR PLAN FOR A SUCCESSFUL WEEK. WHAT WILL YOU DO SO YOU CAN BE YOUR BEST IN THE BIGGEST MOMENTS?

THERE ARE VERY FEW "SURE THINGS" IN LIFE.
NEARLY EVERY OPPORTUNITY WORTH PURSUING WILL CARRY THE
RISK OF FAILURE. HOW DO YOU CALCULATE WHEN THE CHANCE FOR
SUCCESS OUTWEIGHS THE FEAR OF FAILING? TRY IMAGINING YOUR
LIFE IF THE OPPORTUNITY IS A TOTAL SUCCESS. NOW, WHAT DOES
LIFE LOOK LIKE IF THAT SAME OPPORTUNITY IS A COMPLETE
FAILURE? IF THE REWARD IS WORTH THE RISK, ALWAYS BET ON
YOURSELF AND TAKE THE LEAP.

SOMETIMES A WEEK CAN BE A REAL GRIND. BUT THOSE ARE THE WEEKS THAT SHAPE YOU.

THERE WILL ALWAYS BE TENSION AND STRESS IN YOUR PERSONAL AND PROFESSIONAL LIFE. YOU WILL NEED TO MANAGE EGOS, BALANCE PERSONAL TIME WITH YOUR WORKLOAD, AND NAVIGATE UNEXPECTED CHALLENGES. WHAT DID YOU OVERCOME IN THE PAST WEEK THAT MADE YOU A STRONGER AND BETTER PERSON?

SOMETIMES YOU JUST HAVE TO PUT ON YOUR HARD HAT, HEAD INTO THE MINE, AND DO THE DIRTY WORK.

THINK ABOUT SOMETHING YOU NEED TO DO THIS WEEK THAT YOU REALLY DON'T WANT TO DO. WRITE OUT ALL THE WAYS YOU CAN ACCOMPLISH THIS TASK. NOW, CHOOSE THE SIMPLEST PATH AND GET TO WORK.

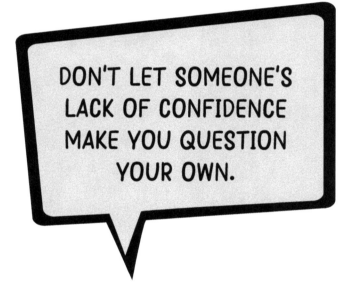

WHEN PEOPLE ARE INSECURE AND SUFFERING, THEY WILL PROJECT THOSE INSECURITIES ONTO YOU. THEY WILL MAKE YOU SUFFER. IT WILL FEEL LIKE THEY ARE WORKING AGAINST YOU. TO COUNTER THIS, WORK ON A PLAN FOR SUCCESS THAT ALSO INCLUDES HOW YOU'RE GOING TO MANAGE THE IMPACT OF THIS PERSON'S INSECURITIES.

HAVE A CHALLENGING PROJECT AHEAD?
USE THIS WEEK'S QUOTE AS YOUR MANTRA TO MAKE
IT TO THE FINISH LINE. NEVER SKIP THE LAST STEP.
EVERY LITTLE "WIN" IS WORTH CELEBRATING!

WEEK 38

PEOPLE WHO ARE
SUFFERING OFTEN JUST NEED
SOMEONE TO SAY,
"I SEE YOU AND I'M LISTENING."

MORE SUFFERING? YES.
THE WORLD IS FILLED WITH ASSHOLES. WE ALL DEAL WITH EMOTIONAL, PHYSICAL, AND MENTAL PAIN. IT'S EASY TO ATTEMPT TO SHIFT THAT PAIN ONTO OTHERS. THIS WEEK, PRACTICE LISTENING. TRUE LISTENING. PICK A PERSON YOU THINK MAY NEED IT AND BE PRESENT FOR THEM. TRULY HEAR THEM. THIS SIMPLE GESTURE CAN HELP THEM PROCESS THEIR PAIN, AND HELP YOU DEVELOP A DEEPER COMPASSION FOR OTHERS.

BEING A PARTNER
MEANS DOING YOUR PART.
BE THERE AND FULLY
COMMIT.

THIS QUOTE IS TRUE WHETHER YOU'RE TALKING ABOUT A LIFE PARTNER, A SPOUSE, OR A WORK PARTNER. YOU HAVE TO BE PREPARED TO ALWAYS GO THE EXTRA MILE FOR THEM. WRITE DOWN SOME IDEAS ON HOW YOU ARE GOING TO SHOW YOUR PARTNER THIS WEEK THAT THEY CAN COUNT ON YOU.

WHEN YOU'RE IN THE MIDDLE OF A PAINFUL EXPERIENCE, REMEMBER THAT PAIN FORCES CHANGE... AND CHANGE FORCES GROWTH.

HUMANS ARE HARDWIRED TO RESIST CHANGE, BUT BEING "STUCK IN YOUR WAYS" WILL LEAVE YOU LIVING A VERY UNFULFILLED LIFE. THIS WEEK, REFLECT ON A RECENT PAINFUL EXPERIENCE. LOOKING BACK NOW, HOW DID THAT NEGATIVE EXPERIENCE FORCE POSITIVE GROWTH IN YOU?

WHEN YOU WAKE UP EACH DAY, YOU HAVE AN IMPORTANT CHOICE TO MAKE: WILL YOU PUT POSITIVE OR NEGATIVE ENERGY OUT INTO THE WORLD?

WE ALL CARRY ENERGY WITHIN US. WHILE SOME PEOPLE LIGHT UP A ROOM, OTHERS CAN DRAG A GATHERING DOWN. NOW, MORE THAN EVER, THE WORLD NEEDS POSITIVE PEOPLE. SO, THIS WEEK, SHARE A SMILE, OFFER A HELPING HAND, OR TRY TO MAKE SOMEONE LAUGH. YOU CAN BE THAT PERSON WHO OTHER PEOPLE MISS WHEN YOUR POSITIVE ENERGY ISN'T AROUND!

WHEN YOU ARE
UNDERTHINKING... READ.
WHEN YOU ARE
OVERTHINKING... WRITE.

CREDIT TO OUR INDIAN YOGI, VIKRAM, FOR THIS ONE.
WHEN YOU'RE BORED, IT IS EASY TO GRAB YOUR PHONE AND
SCROLL THROUGH SOCIAL MEDIA. INSTEAD, TRY PULLING A BOOK
OFF THE SHELF THAT YOU'RE EXCITED TO READ. OR, IF YOUR
MIND IS RACING AND OVERWHELMED WITH THOUGHTS, START
WRITING THEM DOWN. GET THEM OUT ON PAPER SO YOU CAN
ORGANIZE THEM INTO HELPFUL IDEAS.

LET'S BE HONEST, THERE ARE PLENTY OF SHITHEADS OUT THERE. WRITE DOWN EVERYTHING YOU WANT TO SAY TO ONE OF THEM. THEN, GO OUT INTO THE WORLD AND CHOOSE KINDNESS. DO SOMETHING NICE FOR SOMEONE WHO LEAST EXPECTS IT.

A SETBACK IS THE UNIVERSE SAYING, "NOT YET." IT DOESN'T MEAN YOU QUIT. IT MEANS YOU DOUBLE YOUR EFFORTS TO FIND A WAY TO SUCCEED.

THE WORST TIME TO GIVE UP ON SOMETHING IS AFTER A SETBACK. INSTEAD, THIS IS THE PERFECT TIME TO REASSESS, CHANGE DIRECTION, AND PLAN YOUR NEXT STEPS. SOME GOALS ARE EASY TO REACH AND OTHERS TAKE YEARS OF PERSISTENCE AND PATIENCE. WHAT IS A GOAL YOU'RE AFRAID TO TAKE ON BECAUSE YOU THINK IT WILL BE TOO HARD TO ACHIEVE? CAN IT BE BROKEN UP INTO "MINI-GOALS" THAT FEEL MORE DOABLE?

A HEALTHY RELATIONSHIP IS
ONE WHERE BOTH INDIVIDUALS
TRULY VALUE AND CARE
FOR EACH OTHER.

TAKE THIS WEEK TO REFLECT ON THE MOST IMPORTANT
RELATIONSHIP IN YOUR LIFE. EVALUATE THIS RELATIONSHIP.
WHAT ARE YOU DOING WELL? WHAT CAN YOU DO BETTER?
WHAT ARE THE WAYS YOU CAN REMIND THE OTHER PERSON
(OR DOG) THAT YOU VALUE THEM? WRITE THEM ALL DOWN AND
TRY THE FIRST ONE TODAY.

FAR TOO MANY PEOPLE CHOOSE TO BURY THEIR TALENTS IN EXCUSES. "I DON'T HAVE THE TIME... MONEY... SUPPORT TO PURSUE [BLANK]." PLEASE STOP. **YOU ARE CREATIVE.** WHAT IS YOUR TALENT? HOW ARE YOU GOING TO SHARE IT WITH THE REST OF US? MAKE A PLAN!

SELF-AWARENESS IS RECOGNIZING YOUR FLAWS. REAL GROWTH IS TAKING STEPS TOWARD CORRECTING THEM.

WHAT ARE THE TRIGGERS THAT BRING OUT YOUR WORST FLAWS? HOW CAN OTHERS HELP YOU AVOID THOSE TRIGGERS? WRITE DOWN ALL THE WAYS YOU NEED SUPPORT. THEN, HAVE AN OPEN AND HONEST CONVERSATION WITH YOUR LOVED ONES. AN IMPORTANT STEP IN BEING YOUR BEST IS ASKING FOR HELP FROM PEOPLE WHO ONLY WANT TO SEE YOU SUCCEED.

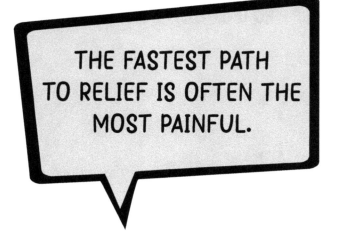

THE FACT OF THE MATTER IS YOU WILL SPEND YOUR ENTIRE LIFE SUFFERING THROUGH SETBACKS. THE GOOD NEWS IS YOU NOW HAVE THE EXPERIENCE TO TACKLE THE MOST PAINFUL ISSUE YOU'VE BEEN AVOIDING. START THE WORK. CONFRONT THE PAIN. MAKE A PLAN FOR HOW TO RESOLVE IT.

WHENEVER YOU PURGE YOUR PHYSICAL, MENTAL, OR EMOTIONAL BAGGAGE, IT SETS YOU FREE TO TAKE BIGGER STEPS FORWARD ON YOUR JOURNEY THROUGH LIFE.

SO MANY OF THE BIGGEST ISSUES WE DEAL WITH IN ADULTHOOD ARE ROOTED IN ISSUES FROM OUR CHILDHOOD. WE SPEND OUR ENTIRE LIVES UNPACKING PHYSICAL, MENTAL, AND EMOTIONAL BAGGAGE FROM OUR FORMATIVE YEARS. WHAT ARE YOU HANGING ONTO FROM YOUR CHILDHOOD THAT MAY BE HOLDING YOU BACK? HOW IS IT IMPACTING YOU NOW? WHAT STEPS CAN YOU TAKE TO HEAL AND MOVE FORWARD?

CATCH IT IN THE ROUGH OR YOU'LL NEED TO FIX IT IN THE FINISH.

THIS IS A MOTTO USED IN CONSTRUCTION,
BUT IT ALSO APPLIES TO LIFE. IF YOU DON'T ADDRESS
SOMETHING EARLY ON, IT'LL BE MORE COSTLY TO DEAL WITH IT
LATER. WHAT IS A PROBLEM YOU ARE AVOIDING BECAUSE YOU'RE
NOT READY TO FACE IT? WHAT IS YOUR PLAN FOR WORKING
TOWARD ADDRESSING THIS PROBLEM?

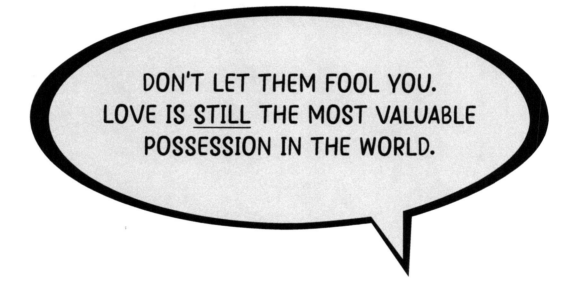

SOCIETY WOULD HAVE YOU BELIEVE THAT MONEY IS WHAT MATTERS MOST. THAT'S BULLSHIT. FINDING YOUR TRUE CALLING IN LIFE IS ANSWERING THE QUESTION, "WHAT DO I LOVE TO DO?" FINDING YOUR LIFE PARTNER IS ANSWERING THE QUESTION, "WILL THIS PERSON LOVE ME UNCONDITIONALLY WHEN I'M AT MY LOWEST?" FINDING HAPPINESS IN LIFE IS GIVING LOVE TO OTHERS FREELY. SO, WHAT AND WHO DO YOU LOVE?

YOU HAVE SPENT THE LAST YEAR WORKING ON YOURSELF. YOU'VE REFLECTED ON LIFE, YOU'VE CHOSEN KINDNESS, AND YOU'VE COMMITTED TO GIVING TO OTHERS IN GENEROUS WAYS. IF YOU WANT TO KNOW HOW FAR YOU'VE COME, JUST LOOK BACK AT WHERE YOU STARTED. THE MOST IMPORTANT PERSON IN YOUR LIFE WILL TAKE NOTICE OF YOUR GROWTH AND LOVE YOU FOR IT.

**THANK YOU FOR GOING ON
THIS JOURNEY OF GROWTH WITH US.**

WE ARE SO VERY PROUD OF YOU!

ARON GAUDET + GITA PULLAPILLY

Husband-and-wife team Aron Gaudet and Gita Pullapilly are award-winning writers, producers, and directors known for their intimate and authentic storytelling. In 2019, Pullapilly was selected as a Presidential Leadership Scholar. In 2016, Gaudet and Pullapilly were awarded the prestigious Guggenheim Fellowship for their work as artists. They are known for their films, *The Way We Get By, Beneath The Harvest Sky,* and *Queenpins.* Prior to working in Hollywood, Gaudet and Pullapilly worked in television news.

Pullapilly received her undergraduate degree in finance from the University of Notre Dame, and her master's degree in journalism from Northwestern University. She was born and raised in South Bend, Indiana. Gaudet received his undergraduate degree from New England School of Communications and grew up in Old Town, Maine. They live in Los Angeles, California with their dog, Miss Minnie Pearl, and their two cats, Jordan and Beanie. *Inspiration To Get You Through a F*cked Up Year* is their first book.

CPSIA information can be obtained
at www.ICGtesting.com
Printed in the USA
BVHW012146191022
649879BV00010B/197

9 780940 121997